ODD MAN OUT FIGHTING FOR VISIBILITY IN CORPORATE AMERICA

Gary L. Garris

ISBN 9780989057318

Library of Congress Control Number: 2013934737

I dedicate this book to my wife Cecily and my children Danielle, Alex and Brandon. Thanks to my mom, Audrey and my sister, Yvette for putting up with my nonsense over the years and to my beloved brother Vic, you are missed and I carry you in my heart every day. I stand on your shoulders little bro. To my mother-in-law who happens to be the coolest video gamer I know.

Finally, to my dad, John, Grandfather, James and Grandmother Lillie a legacy of struggle, perseverance and hard work are the real ties that bind. Missed, but never forgotten.

Table of Contents

ODD MAN OUT

FIGHTING FOR VISIBILITY IN CORPORATE AMERICA

Acknowledgements

Where do I start? I guess with the people who loved me enough to endure every story, every moment of drama in which I made a call or a visit to try to cope with work challenges that I often encountered and still do to this day.

Some of the advice that follows is a testament to guidance provided from those who had more of a vested interest in my well being than in my success in the workplace.

In many cases our loved ones often help to bridge that divide between what our mentors want us to become and who we really are; the two at times, being more mutually exclusive than not.

To all past, present and future co-workers and employers thank you for the opportunity to learn, grow and change in my pursuit of all things work related. I have travelled to many places and visited many sites that would not have otherwise been possible. Special thanks to Frank Corrado, a fantastic guidance counselor out of Eastside High School in Paterson, New Jersey and the best High School Principal known to man, Joe Clark.

Finally, to my children, Danielle, Alex and Brandon I wish for you a life in which you are seen and heard. A life filled with the proper perspectives and values that allow you to define your own career path free from insecurity, doubt, frustration and rejection that so many others feel in the workplace. Never give up. Never surrender.

Foreword

While I have written this book from the perspective of an African-American male trying to overcome the challenges of succeeding in Corporate America, it applies to anyone who longs for success in a place where you are different from many. Maybe in thought, behavior, or beliefs you have found yourself on the outside looking in and wondering how you can become more relevant in the workplace.

Before you invest a great deal of your time reading further, I want to explain what has led me to this place, if you will. After twenty plus years of working in the corporate arena, I found that I was spending the last several years of my career dispensing guidance to many of my peers centered for the most part on how to overcome some type of barrier or perceived obstacle to their career goals and aspirations.

At times, I really felt like a guidance counselor; coaching people on how to handle almost every conceivable challenge anyone could think up at work. I drafted countless resumes and actively pursued opportunities on behalf of dozens of associates spanning the last twenty years.

I became frustrated with the extreme discussions and debates that I had with people who asked for advice but did not possess the ability to step out of the situation and take the advice that was given.

They wanted to wallow in a place that I could not relate to, sort of a corporate graveyard where people who burnout or become too angry, go to die. A place that is difficult to recover from once you get there and certainly impossible to escape from without an ability to look inward.

I decided to see if I could encapsulate some meaningful guidance for those who are still receptive to perhaps a different way of thinking when it comes to managing through the many challenges associated with working in the corporate arena.

While everyone can certainly learn some valuable lessons in this book, I focus primarily on the particular challenges that

African-Americans have in the workplace and the steps that can be taken to get to a better place.

Before we start, keep in mind that everyone cannot be a CEO, Executive or even a Manager for that matter but if you read on I am confident that you will gain some additional tools to help you maneuver through the pitfalls. Also, I keep it real in this book so if you think this is going to be about what others need to do in order for you to succeed, you might want to look for an alternative source for career guidance.

Chapter 1

Tie That Binds

I will never forget that hot humid day in August when I walked into a college class for the first time and I was late. I compounded the problem by spending too much time looking for a seat. The professor waited for me to sit and he asked me to explain why I picked that particular seat. It was bad enough that I was taking college courses in the summer but to have to be the first one called on as sweat was dripping from my face made it even worse.

I gave him an answer that would start a dialogue that lasted the entire summer. I gave him the answer that he sought in a way that I was sure would secure an A in that course. "I picked this seat because this is the side of the class where all the Black people are sitting", I exclaimed. Half of the class laughed and the other half looked confused. The professor then asked me if I personally knew any of the Black people around me and I looked around and said "no I do not".

To be fair, he did pose the same question to my White counterparts and then to a few Asians in the class, as well. Unfortunately for me, no one really provided a self reflective reason that held the professor's interest except for yours truly. So we went one on one for an hour as I explained my seat selection, first starting out by saying that "it's the tie that binds".

Explaining that I share a common bond with a group of people forged by negative and positive experiences that provides some degree of comfort and acceptance that I did not believe existed on the other side of the room, hence my seat selection. "So you are making an assumption about another race" was his response.

"No I am making a statement of fact about my race" was the retort. Yeah, I was kind of radical back then or at least I thought so. Keep in mind the summer of 1984 was filled with racial strife in our urban cities and many college campuses were dealing with challenges to divest from South Africa so I had a bit of a chip on my shoulder and I was waiting for someone to knock it off.

It was the kind of class that continued long after it was over, people gathering outside on the lawn openly discussing the subject matter in small groups. When White students opened up it became even more exciting. They challenged Black students to move beyond the pain caused by their ancestors, to let down their guard and trust that they were different, that they were not the keepers of their forefathers' past.

For Black students, our "yeah right" sort of sarcastic response to the argument the past is the past did not resonate coming from people who could not relate to the daily challenges that we continued to face. Poverty, police brutality, lapses in education etc. are all recurring themes that continue to play out now, decades later.

Eventually the professor was able to bring the disparate groups together by first getting us to acknowledge our differences. He then got us to focus on building a common and shared belief system without regard to any personal limitations or bias that we had set for ourselves or others.

In the end, that classroom became integrated, not just because we openly discussed our issues and challenges, but we also did something about them. We stepped outside of our comfort zone and took a chance by becoming more inclusive and tolerant of different ideas and opinions.

In order to get there we had to whittle away at deeply seeded notions that were reinforced by stereotypes that others taught us to believe. We started by looking into the past and then quickly looked to move to the present and ultimately the future. That class was worth it, we didn't solve world peace but I gained a healthy respect for people who did not look like me and I started down my colloquial path with a much more open mind towards the future.

Sometimes the pain of the past for many, becomes a place of solace, that when revisited too often, gives comfort to present day circumstances filled with shortcomings and personal failures that we often, rightly or wrongly, attribute to others.

For Blacks in this country, we simply cannot afford to stay in that place for too long; no matter how justified we may be in doing so, because it prevents us from ascending to a higher place. A place where our fears and suspicions fall to our hopes and aspirations and our tepidness is replaced with the possibility of something grander.

In Corporate America, much like that class, we must first deconstruct the obstacles that we have placed on ourselves by first understanding and acknowledging our challenges and then by building a shared path that focuses on managing around or through the obstacles that prevent us from moving up that hypothetical career ladder.

More and more of us are moving away from pursuing opportunities in the corporate arena opting to establish our own businesses as a means of gaining economic independence and a sense of control over one's destiny. However, for the vast majority of us, the corporate arena remains the battleground of choice or necessity for employment.

Whatever choice you make, the hurdles will always be there some, of which are formed based on the wrong assumptions about your motivations, intent, and capability; in addition to any personal doubts, anxieties or misguided notions that you also bring to the table.

Our reaction to hurdles that get in the way of our career goals is more important than any particular obstacle that we may face at any given time. In the case of African Americans, our reactions are almost always universally damaging when it comes to dealing with career challenges where we suspect bias or discrimination.

I have seen it all too often and I have found myself teetering on the brink of falling into that vicious cycle of them versus us, myself. You know that place you go to for comfort when things don't go your way at work. The boss is incompetent, bias, or just plain ignorant. Whatever the rationale, the focus tends to be everywhere except on you.

Even in instances where our worst suspicions are valid, we react in a way that gets us to the wrong place more times than not. We spend too much time looking to others to validate our self worth. Hoping that if we do a good job, someone will notice and you will get the raise or promotion you seek. And when that doesn't happen we revert back to negative thinking.

Remember, my answer to the professor spoke to both positive and negative experiences that bind Blacks together. If you thought that I was referring solely to those experiences associated with dealing with Whites, you are sadly mistaken.

We bring our own negative counterproductive thought processes to the mix, which only fuels the fire and keeps us trapped in a perpetual cycle of frustration and disappointment as we look to validate ourselves through the eyes of others. So the proverbial "tie" serves a dual purpose, it can give a sense of protection and support or it can be constraining or limiting when relied on incorrectly.

In order to move forward we must really look at the things that hold us back and address them head on. For me, the tie that bound at times felt like a knot. You know, those really tough tight knots that no matter how many times you try to loosen, in the end, the outcome is always the same, it stays stuck. It took awhile to get to a place where I learned to avoid making the knot too tight or getting too caught up in my personal web of frustration and anger.

Think about the analogy for a moment. When you untie your laces with one pull of the string the laces go in every direction possible. But they are still the same laces made with the same material that you will see and touch over and over again. We should use our life's lessons to help us avoid getting stuck in a sort of proverbial career knot. Be multi-dimensional in taking stock of your career goals and aspirations.

Don't get locked into linear thinking that keeps you on a self fulfilling path that ends up constraining you in a way that contributes to a realization of the same undesired results.

Above all else one should perceive change and challenge as an opportunity. Even if your immediate reaction is fear and trepidation, try and push that back with a more forward thinking look at what you are facing.

Chapter 2

I Am Hired Hear Me Roar

Sure, there is nothing like getting that job to boost the confidence and sense of self esteem that comes with a new assignment. "Let me show you to your office, follow me" the administrative assistant says. Now let me ask what are you doing as you walk down the corridor to your new workplace home? You are doing the same thing I did in that class, "how many of us are here", "did I see one of us in a big office" you say to yourself.

As you attempt to get comfortable and build a support network remember that sometimes the rules of life apply a little differently to you. For many, it may be "who you know" that gets you to the next level but for people of color, you are always going to have to first demonstrate "what you know". So make sure you actually learn something before you start looking to take over your boss' job.

For our young ladies and gentlemen entering the workforce for the first time please make sure that you are dressing for the workplace and not the club. Appropriate attire usually does not garner much attention but inappropriate dress can quickly become a focus in the organization. Garner the right kind of attention by remaining professional and focused.

How you dress and behave is being examined in the workplace at all times. The buddy that you are going to lunch with who is on the fast track to becoming a superstar may be able to wear those faded jeans on Friday, but you might be perceived differently if you choose to do so and that is simply a fact of life. Be in the moment, make choices that you are comfortable with but be aware of the potential ramifications of those choices as you carry them out.

Always seek to counteract negative or bias perceptions by ensuring that everything that you do is counter to any potential bad press that may be aimed at you. This will have long benefits down the road when you come across associates who might speak out of turn or for you when you are not present. One of the games that often gets played in the corporate arena is the "I'll speak for you game". I can't tell you how many times someone took an innocent statement that someone else may have said and went back to the boss to curry favor and ended up sending people down the river.

For every one person who thinks it's about working hard and staying focused, remember that there are nine others who want to get there at someone else's expense. Don't obsess over what someone is saying about you when you are not around, just make sure that what you do at work remains professional and focused at all times. If the boss encounters some third or 4th party criticism of you it will be in direct contrast to what they see and hear everyday which will make that kind of feedback suspect.

Even though it's about what we know, especially early in our careers, I have to admit that who you know determines what you know at times. So make sure you surround yourself with people who know the business and are willing to provide you with relevant insight into what's going on. However, one should not solely rely on those relationships to advance in an organization. Leverage them for expanding your knowledge and exposure to different scenarios and making friends. At the end of the day, it still needs to be about what you know first and foremost.

Sometimes in our quest to demonstrate what we know, we feel that we have to opine on every comment made in a meeting. No one likes know-it-alls and it's ok to let people bask in their own ignorance, if it doesn't jeopardize an objective or presents a risk to the company. Meetings would be cut in half if people didn't try to one up each other and just focused on getting the work done. I recall attending lunch with a group of people who were with the company for quite some time.

They started reminiscing about the good old days recalling the time when lunch was free and you got paid a meal allowance when you stayed late. "Yes", you heard me correctly, lunch was free and there were break rooms with pool tables and TVs during the prehistoric 1980s. Nevertheless, they went on for what seemed like an eternity about perks that didn't really seem to be that important.

Yet there was something unique about what I observed, as I looked around the table it was almost familial. I saw decades of history and experience and maybe a few battle scars from people who were part of a living and breathing institution. People that helped the company survive, thrive and even grow.

I didn't walk away from that lunch with any real appreciation for those perks of yester year but I did glean some insight into how important it is to demonstrate respect for those who came before you. Very much in the same way that your parents taught you to do the same for family elders, you should do the same for those in the workplace as well.

Your Excel spreadsheets or Access databases may run circles around that calculator that the senior associate is using, but remember, the actual methodology that you used to come up with those formulas was probably developed by those who came before you.

Bringing others up to the 21st century from a technology perspective might prove challenging but extending a hand is not only personally fulfilling, but a responsibility that cuts across any sort of artificial divide that might exist. This is what I mean by being-in-the-moment. Do not be so quick to discount people or situations without stepping outside of where you are and examining it from an objective vantage point.

My lunch sessions with those senior employees gave me some valuable insight into how to overcome some of the challenges I encountered when I had to change work processes that impacted them. I learned about the undocumented processes, political challenges and technical aspects of the organization that are not usually visible to an outsider. It made a big differences in how I was perceived by management and when I made a mistake or two along the way I had the support of those who came before me because they knew how much I cared about getting it right. If you only see your job as just a job, then you probably would have never picked up this book.

For those of you with less than 5 years work experience, you should be spending that time learning the business and focusing on any formal educational goals that remain outstanding. A little difficult to do those things once the spouse and a few offspring start showing up so you should plan accordingly.

Before I move to the next chapter I have to tell you about a story of a young lady that reported to me in a previous life.

She had a solid background in technology and a personable demeanor that I thought would make for a good fit in the company. What I didn't realize was that she quickly wanted me out of the way as well as my boss and wanted to spend time with the senior executive of the group.

To make it a short story, I tried to rein her in a bit in a one on one meeting suggesting that she might want to consider running her proposals if not by me, at least my boss before going to the next level. I honestly don't think she actually saw me until I criticized her. In her mind I was transparent. She immediately looked beyond me, through me, as if my guidance and opinion didn't matter.

I genuinely believe that she displayed an almost entitlement mindset to what she deserved in relation to me. I am not saying that she consciously exhibited any sort of racial bias but I do believe that she discounted my opinion, experience and guidance outright because her subconscious belief system taught her that she should not be subordinate to a person of color. But I stayed in the moment and after a few probing questions realized that she desperately wanted a promotion after 120 days on the job.

Moreover, such a promotion would never come from me because I was not high enough in rank from her perspective. So was it about race or was it more about the person being a jerk? After many years in the workplace, I now realize that she would have behaved that way if I was as white as snow.

We ended the discussion soon thereafter and I did what every good employee does, I made sure my boss knew about the situation and when all efforts to get her to reconsider the approach failed, I suggested that she take her proposals to the proverbial mountain top of leadership if she so desired.

My point here is that you have to pick and choose your battles in the workplace and they should be rare and done with the utmost professionalism. After all most of us have the same aspirations and dreams, the differences often lie in how we pursue and hold onto them.

Don't believe that good guys finish last; you can still hold onto your sense of self and do the right thing. While some may rely on familial relationships and connections to gain advantage those shortcuts can have a downside as well.

Life is too short to be consumed by the pursuit of titles or a false sense of power.

Do the job to the best of your ability and keep the right balance and perspective. Never let the job define who you are, self worth should be about more important things than the job. For those of you who have been working for awhile just consider this chapter a refresher and for others who may feel like I am not delving deep enough into the particular issues that people of color face in climbing up the career ladder – read on.

Chapter 3

Black Like Who

If you can't tell by now I am writing and engaging you from the perspective of a mentor who has been around the block once or twice. Someone who has learned a lot from people who shared their lessons learned and presented me with an opportunity or two along the way. They were all good people who had a tremendous background and solid professional record of achievement. Every single one of them happened to be White which is another reason why I decided to write this book.

My history does not have to be yours but let me share some of my experiences with Executives in Corporate America who happened to be Black. First and foremost, they happen to be few and far between. When you look across the landscape and if you take those who are in Human Resources out of the calculation you will probably lose at least 1/3 in the count.

Now imagine what it really takes to get to that level. Hard work, determination and persistency probably would not be enough to get there. It takes more than many of us can imagine. So once we arrive and we become part of the club, our entire focus is centered on making sure we stay. We have to ingratiate ourselves to Whites to ensure that those relationships and opportunities keep coming.

So when we approach someone in an Executive position who may look like us we revert back to that class. Yes, that class is back again. We start going back to the tie that binds mentality that raises expectations and our comfort level so we step forward reach out and go for it. Guess what folks? There is a tie that binds but the shoelace is on the other foot this time around. Too many of us upon arrival to the corporate promise land spend too much time walking a sort of self-imposed tightrope centered on disproving any sort of allegiance to race.

It is quite frankly a standard that Whites do not have to bare in fact, it is quite the opposite. Cousins, in-laws, friends are all welcome to the table in their world. One in which they actively seek out opportunities and advance individuals at various levels in the organization.

So why can't we do the same? Well for one, we don't feel empowered to do so and we are still hampered by the house versus field Negro mentality of yester year. We bought into the idea that only one or two of us can get there, but that is about it when it comes to advancing to the upper echelon of Corporate America. Sure we feel comfortable reaching back into the community and helping young people focus on the fundamentals because that doesn't entrench on our sense of territory but God forbid a peer approaches you about opportunities where you work; we start ducking and diving as quickly as possible.

I recall being introduced to a Black executive who happened to be an attorney by my boss who wanted to demonstrate how the company really embraces diversity. He stood up smiling and shining in front of my boss suggesting that we get together to discuss how wonderful the company is and compare notes. I still remember him shining as we left the office. "Make sure you reach out" he said, "will do" I exclaimed.

I called him up a week later to suggest lunch and his exact quote was "ok but I can't give you no job or anything". Gone was the corporate vernacular that he so eloquently displayed in front of my boss. On full display was the house Negro afraid that I might pull him off his tightrope. I won't delve into the details of what transpired during that discussion but suffice it to say I referenced his use of Ebonics and a few other things and then moved on.

While I know that the vast majority of Blacks in leadership positions in Corporate America are not like this, too many of us are and that needs to change. I am not sure what drives that type of behavior. Maybe we spend too much of the paycheck on living the life and then we go to extreme measures to protect those assets once we get to a certain level. Maybe there is some sort of unspoken pressure from White America to prove that you are race neutral in all that you do. I have to admit that I have been pre-empted a few times when I wanted to promote, hire or reward people of color and found myself fighting above and beyond to prove their worth to superiors.

My point is that we have to not just be concerned with how White America sees us at work but also how we see each other. I recall standing on the floor having an impromptu discussion with two white Executives, myself and a young man that I was mentoring who happened to be Black. In the course of the discussion I told a joke about something my mentee did that caused everyone to break up with laughter and as my mentee laughed he called me the "N word" because I was giving him a hard time, if you will.

The laughter stopped and the two White gentlemen looked directly at me to see how I would react. I dropped my head in embarrassment, ended the discussion abruptly and asked the mentee to follow me to a conference room. I closed the door and he said "I know, I know I realized what I said as soon as it came out" what I could not understand at the time was why he would ever result to using the word in first place. He was reprimanded verbally and advised that if I ever heard him use the word again, appropriate disciplinary action would soon follow along with my foot in an uncomfortable place.

For the record I consider the word to be hateful, ignorant and repulsive on many levels. If you use it, stop. Can you imagine watching your child being born in the hospital and you exclaim "I love that little n****" or you bend down on one knee and say "n**** will you marry me".

No matter how you try to explain away its use and adoption within the Black community it still ends up being the ultimate display of hypocrisy on our part. There is a certain duality about being Black in Corporate America. Especially for those of us who came from the heart of the ghetto. Somehow you have to make that transition from the hood to mainstream America in the way you walk and talk both literally and figuratively.

Some of those who grew up in the Black middle class may have to make the same adjustments but I would contend that they have a leg up for the most part. For others like me, the struggle can at times prove to be maddening but I would not have had it any other way.

There is a certain vibe, flow or style that comes with being Black in America. A kind of in the mix, above the fray, keep moving kind of thing that is hard to put your arms around but you can feel it. How much of us do we get to keep as we continue to assimilate to a standard of neutrality in the workplace remains to be seen but I'm optimistic that we can be who we are and successfully coexist in the workplace.

I recall a young Black man who was born in New York lecturing me on how people from the islands are more successful in this country than American born Blacks. I am not sure why he decided to make those comments to me but I found it intriguing to say the least. I decided to reach out to a few friends who happened to be from the Caribbean to get their perspective on the comments and to my surprise they agreed. I opted against an all out debate at the time because I thought it would be counterproductive. I must admit I get a little tired of people coming to this country and immediately elevating themselves above those born here, especially above Americans who happen to be Black.

What I did learn from the exchange is that those support mechanisms that we rely on such as race, skin color, nationality etc. might not be the right ones to hold onto. Maybe the tie that binds is driven by collective experiences and shared histories that cut across the stereotypes and pre-conceptions that we place on others in order to feel better about where we are at any given time. If we can form sort of these compartmentalize biases amongst ourselves, then who are we, to complain about what Whites might be saying.

At the end of the day we should continue to discuss debate and challenge each other without marginalizing our respective strengths and experiences in a way that makes it easier for the next person who needs to travel down that proverbial path to a rewarding career.

Our definition of self needs to move beyond the typical groupthink cliquish mentality that is pervasive in our communities and allow for more divergent positive viewpoints on what being Black is all about. And yes, that should include input from others because it is not just about how we perceive ourselves that counts. We must also understand how our actions are perceived by others, as well so read on.

Chapter 4

Is It Us or Them?

Sometimes the expectations are so low that you have to stop and wonder how people really see you in the workplace or whether they see you at all. The subtle personal questions that people sometimes pose to gain a better understanding of who you are and what you represent is because in all likelihood you exceeded their expectations.

In essence, there can be and often is something suspect about you and it shows up in varying ways. The "where are you from" and "you are so articulate" kind of comments that are intended to be complimentary but end up offending many of us can be too much sometimes.

Remember that our experiences are common. I contend that they are almost parallel in many ways when it comes to working in Corporate America. The question to ask is whether or not we should have that sort of insular reaction to what amounts to a genuine attempt to pay you a compliment. These sort of minor transgressions from Whites in the workplace tend to feed the idea or notion that they are insensitive to diversity and lack a real connection to people who are different. But is that really the case?

If the only contact that White people use to define their perception of Blacks in this country centers around rap videos, sitcoms and stereotypes handed down from generation to generation. What can you expect the reaction to be if they rarely come into contact with someone different from the images portrayed in the media? Where is Bill Cosby when you need him?

I am still amazed at how many of my White peers spend their existence in an exclusively homogeneous environment that unintentionally shuts out people who are different. Imagine getting up and spending your day without encountering or engaging Whites. Almost impossible for Blacks but for many Whites, outside of encountering us in a service capacity at a restaurant or store, their lives still play out in a relatively homogeneous environment.

I submit that in the workplace we are invisible, rarely seen and even more importantly rarely heard when it comes to opinions and insight about the organization – in essence, invisible. The Black executive or two that shows promise by building the correct relationships typically ends up in an HR role as opposed to a business leadership opportunity on the front lines. All too common for comfort from where I sit.

It is disheartening to look around the landscape and see Executives that look like me relegated to non critical business functions. Although many Black Executives in the field might disagree with me on this topic I would submit that in the aggregate a disproportionate share of us wind up in Human Resources as opposed to CEO, CIO or COO positions in Corporate America.

I am not knocking Human Resources at all but I, along with many colleagues, have noticed that quite a number of Executives in large organizations who happen to be Black are housed in Human Resources or a support function as opposed to a front line assignment like Sales, Finance or Technology.

Let's face it, sometimes the fundamental questions that we have to deal with centers on our ability to lead organizations, our level of competency and perceptions about motives. It isn't a matter of whether or not we can lead but rather, who will follow. The stigma of affirmative action and underlying tones of prejudice can often make for a poisonous mixture of doubt, mutiny and no confidence from those under your stewardship.

I recall interviewing with a senior Executive for a leadership position who must have repeated you are so articulate a dozen times or so as if he was in disbelief. We never really got to talk about my industry knowledge or why he should hire me for the position versus my competition because he was too busy critiquing my oratory skills. Sure I was frustrated because we didn't focus on what I brought to the table, but I made sure that I was in the moment observing his mannerisms and behavior and looking for tells.

You know what I mean, those little quirks or signs that reveal what people really feel or think in a given situation. I call them tells. At the end of the day and for whatever reason, he was impressed with the way I handled myself during the discussion. He offered me the job after a few more interviews, and I gladly accepted not because of his impression of me, but because his tells indicated his sincerity in thought and deed. Sometimes people mean well even if their delivery is a little off so avoid a rush to judgment.

Being in the moment is about objective observation of the situation as it presents itself without first reverting to charges of racism or bias, even if you can see it and touch it, or it sees and touches you and you know that it is there. How many of us have walked away from jobs or careers because we could not see a way through a particular dilemma? Maybe out of anger, frustration or a sense of hopelessness we chalked it up to racism and moved on to the next job.

I did go back and ask one of my friends who happened to be White what he thought about the Executive's repeated references to me being articulate and his response was telling. "Gary, it's because when we are on those conference calls no one can tell that you are Black, you sound like a White guy", he said. I appreciated his honesty but noted that he really had no idea what he was saying. His own bias on display in its full glory, but it was sort of this naïveté to his comment that made me second guess whether or not my initial anger was warranted or whether or not I needed to give him a pass because he didn't know any better.

These sort of internal debates that we struggle with are often intense and become a point of distraction for us as we attempt to advance up the career ladder. We sometimes find ourselves working overtime to not pull out the race card. Searching for what we did or didn't do to contribute to someone else's bias. I submit that we do too much soul searching in this space and we need to move on by focusing on what we need to do to successfully execute against a strategy that gets us to the next step in our careers.

Sometimes the strategy has to include a way out or around a given situation and may require a series of lateral moves to get where you want to be. Maybe not what you want to hear but there are no laws on the books nor any complaint to HR that will or should get you there. Discrimination exists in the workplace make no mistake about it but the key is to not become so consumed by your experiences that it takes away from your pursuit of excellence in everything you do.

If you look to others to validate your sense of worth then you are already setting yourself up to fail. I don't necessarily think that my positive interactions with leaders who happened to be White were unique by any standard. It was rather, how I chose to deal with a few leaders that I saw as patently biased in the workplace. The gamesmanship, poor assignments and lack of support required that I develop a short term plan to ensure that I successfully executed against their deliverables while building a long term plan to confront them head on or to move on.

If you take a negative experience and typecast all Whites in that regard, how are you any different from what you are accusing others of being? The answer posed by the title of this chapter is quite simply, the individual. Deal with the person(s) but don't take down a whole race of people based on a few lost souls.

In the next chapter we will examine the corporate infrastructure that we see in some organizations when it comes to diversity in the workplace and some of the opportunities to be leveraged from a career development perspective.

Chapter 5

Diversity in the Workplace

Let's assume for the moment that you are a fairly well adjusted solid performer at work and you have mastered the fundamentals on behavior, attitude and competency. You belong to a company that ranks nationally as one of the best companies to work for from a diversity perspective.

After making all the right moves and networking with the right people you still find yourself a level or two away from where you want to be or where you feel you should be. We start to experience disconnects between what the company says and the realities that you observe every day.

While saying it doesn't make it so, many companies follow a cookie cutter approach to getting listed in magazines and websites that focus on diversity but fail to mention the fact that they sponsor or pay consultative fees to some of those organizations to conduct an assessment or evaluation of the company's worthiness for inclusion. Needless to say, every company will say that diversity is a core business mantra in today's environment but you have to look for signs that they back up that message with meaningful opportunities for growth and advancement. Some companies are better at this than others.

A major challenge for Blacks in this regard actually lies with a fundamental change in the demographics of the country for the last 20 years. While diversity and inclusion arose out of a direct fight for equality associated with the Civil Rights movement along with affirmative action programs aimed at increasing Black representation on a number of fronts, it is no longer just a Black and White issue.

Blacks were inserted into companies across the country at all levels to ensure conformance with EEOC mandates and to avoid the stigma of non compliance. Fast tracked for advanced positions and heavily recruited by many, we began to see advancements in education, hiring and promotions for Blacks across the country.

Well other groups have sought and are still seeking those same opportunities today which, makes the game all together different. One cannot simply look at how many Black faces they see in corporate America and draw a conclusion either way regarding whether a company has a solid diversity program. It is more complicated than that and requires observation on many fronts. Suffice it to say that Blacks are no longer the "chosen ones" when it comes to diversity in the workplace. Martin Luther King's dream was all inclusive and the prize is for everyone to share in based on universal fairness.

Evaluating a company's diversity program up close and personal will require that you know someone who is an employee or you have to become an employee sort of after the fact. What you should be looking for are not the cultural activities the company sponsors. For instance, activities that focus on food, dress and casual observances of one's ethnicity heritage etc. are nice things for the company to do but that is not reflective of true corporate diversity programs. We saw those kinds of programs in the 70s and 80s when companies were not exactly sure what they should do to make the workplace more inclusive.

The reality is that we have moved beyond being inclusive. The country continues to be integrated each and every day and while some may seek to stay in an exclusive homogeneous environment, such an effort is defined more and more by class and less by race. Yet company affinity programs and activities around diversity continue to focus on bridging the cultural divide versus the opportunity divide that still exists in the workplace.

These programs need to be more focused on the specific skill-sets that need to be acquired for advancement and growth opportunities in the company along with programs that break down stereotypes and misconceptions of hiring and promoting managers as it relates to people of color.

The vast majority of people in these positions of authority are White and the company has a moral and legal obligation to affirmatively ensure that opportunity for all Americans is a real possibility not just in entry level positions but also in the middle and senior levels of management, as well.

Because we sometimes enter the workplace with this sort of utopist idea that if we work really hard someone will notice us and we will eventually advance, it becomes difficult for us to recognize when we need to change our course of action and become more actively engaged in seeking out opportunities.

For example, one might want to keep that worker bee in a given position and pay them bonuses and thank them constantly for a job well done but might not look to promote them elsewhere because they excel at that particular job. You have to know when to get off the bus as opposed to staying on and asking are we there yet. You may find that you will never get to your destination.

If you listen to some Black leaders who have made it in Corporate America, you will sometimes hear them challenge you to network and get out and about and meet people who might one day be in a position to do something for you down the road.

Of course, you can't just say hello how are you, can I get a hook up. It doesn't quite work that way, certainly not for us. So if you come across an industry article or topic of interest, sharing that with mentors or leaders can demonstrate business acumen and a desire to grow and learn. Or seeking out input about a training class that you are thinking about can demonstrate respect for that particular leader's opinion which can foster trust, as well.

While networking is a positive means that might lead to opportunities down the road, it is a very difficult thing for many of us to pull off. I sometimes wonder if we don't show up in the upper ranks of companies because of our uneasiness or lack of comfort with befriending Whites in the workplace. I can certainly relate to the "work is work and my personal life is my personal life" mantra that so many of us espouse to, and rightfully so.

After all we tend to hold our personal life sacrosanct from all things work. But maybe being overprotective about our personal lives is a bit counterproductive. After all I have friends and neighbors who happen to be White so why can't I also have the same relationships in the workplace? I call it the kissing ass dilemma. It is this sort of uneasiness that we have about receiving rewards or benefiting from relationships with Whites that might cause us to questions our blackness. After all, who wants to be a sell-out?

In essence, we don't really want to advance or receive opportunities unless we have earned them and we are qualified. Trying to fight against the stigma of preferential treatment in the workplace and the notion by some, of an unearned or illegitimate assignment, we bend over backwards to hold ourselves to a higher standard in that regard when others don't.

How many times have we heard from our parents that we have to be twice as good to hold the same job? Maybe it was a way of encouraging us to hang in there and pursue excellence peppered with some truth for reality sake.

I guess what I want the reader to walk away with from in this chapter is an understanding of the conflicting feelings that we have to deal with in the workplace when it comes to supporting advancement of not only ourselves but other minority groups as well. If you were not worthy of the opportunity it probably would not have been extended in the first place. Moving beyond adherence to a false doctrine of what it means to be Black will free you from the trepidation that can sometimes come with success. If it's there reach out and grab it.

Chapter 6

Affirmative Action Whose Party Is It?

No matter what side you come down on, affirmative action is still very much a hot button issue in America. While I detest the stigma that comes with the implication that Blacks entering the workplace are *given* jobs that belong to Whites. I deplore the entitlement mindset that some people have even more. Even if 10% of jobs were set aside for minorities based solely on race, the 90% of jobs that go to Whites is still not enough?

The reality is that affirmative action benefits Whites as well. White women now have the opportunity to join Corporate America in senior leadership positions. I am still not convinced that minorities benefit to the detriment of Whites in the aggregate. The issue is complex but demonizing others, in particular White men is certainly not the answer.

Nevertheless, it's a debate that we must have because the need for finding a way to address the significant disparities brought on by the racist past of our forefathers should not come at the real or perceived expense of others. The current solution is an imperfect attempt to right a wrong that perpetuates an undeniable stigma that we can also do without.

As a member of the corporate community the best thing that you can do is display exemplary performance in all that you do each and every step along the way. Staying mired in the muck of race and its implications only draws you away from what your true purpose should be in the workplace.

Especially if there are some who have decided to have lower expectations because of what you look like. Use that to your advantage by blasting their socks off with your intellect, passion for the business and of course, your professionalism.

While it's disheartening to see the comparative studies that often show Whites significantly outscoring minorities on aptitude tests, we must apply the proper perspective. After all, if you were White and you saw tests scores that showed your race outperforms other races consistently in these types of tests, you would feel superior. While we all know the causal factors that lead to this feeling of superiority and entitlement by some, we must find ways to overcome the perception that we bring less to the table then others. Instead of wasting time playing this sort of racial dalliance seeking to explain disparities why not simply seek to be magnificently excellent in what you do.

Remember the old adage that I referred to earlier that many of us grew up hearing; "you have to be twice as good" just to get a basic entry level job. Easier said than done in an increasingly polarizing society that is drawn along racial and ethnic lines at the expense of true societal progress. But the reality is that no one is going to care about that in the workplace so here is what you need to do.

Five years into the job you should have at least an advanced degree and at least a certification or expert designation in one required skill-set for what you do. If you don't have a degree, you should shoot for that as the primary goal and look to obtain a degree from an accredited institution that supports students who also work full-time.

Hard work can make up for lost time associated with being caught up in a racial vortex of frustration, anger, resentment and hatred so focus on fulfillment of self above those things that can eat away at you.

It is not about how much discourse and frustration you can take, but how much of you that is sacrificed following down a path that leads to nowhere. Our fight is not with others but rather within oneself to focus on improvement and growth in the workplace.

I am not dismissing the fact that the color of your skin sometimes plays a role in the hand that you are dealt in the workplace, it does. But finding a place where one can get to that allows for a refocus on ways to overcome those obstacles should be what the mission is about.

I remember showing up at an open house for new condos with my soon to be wife after being told of vacancies in a particular New Jersey town. We showed up and all of a sudden the vacancies dried up. We of course went home called the next day and were told that there were plenty of vacancies.

My friends at work could not believe it. A buddy of mine went so far as to visit the development and was offered an application and shown several open units. Of course my friend happened to be White. Then another friend did the same thing and it became a big focus at work. My White friends looked embarrassed for us and some were angry at the outcome.

While I was disappointed that my fiancé at the time was upset and hurt by the experience I quickly came to the conclusion that I did not want to live where I was not wanted and moved on. Sometimes the fight is not worth the toll.

Life is too short. Someone else's problem is just that - so stay positive and keep pushing. We should not rely on the government to affirmatively address or resolve workplace discrimination and bias or see them in a primary role in the fight for fairness and opportunity in the workplace.

Frankly it is in everyone's interest to level the playing field and foster partnership, access and transparency in how individuals are recruited and promoted in the organization.

The most significant challenge that we have in the workplace is one of access and opportunity. Imagine trying to lead in an environment where you are suspect by some in terms of capability and experience. Sure White managers go through the same thing but when that doubt and suspicion is tinged by race it can get you mired in a soup of frustration and anger as you seek to maneuver through obstacle after obstacle.

My grandmother used to say you have to make do with what you have and I guess that was truly the mantra for so many that came before us. However, I am frankly sick and tired of just making do and so are a whole lot of others. We need to become passionate advocates for tolerance, acceptance, access and opportunity in the workplace. We have to own it, not the government either as employees or consumers or both.

You will find that many companies attempt to launch multicultural campaigns by going into our communities extolling the virtues of diversity and sponsoring events that are likely to draw a high rate of minority attendance. However, when you look across the organization, we are represented in a fraction of leadership positions yet we are expected to purchase products and services from a company representative who looks like us. Many companies just don't get it. If you want to diversify your consumer base in a real, sustainable and profitable way, you have to start with your employee base.

That is the fastest way to make gains from a multicultural marketing perspective. Our role as consumers can also play a powerful role in the workplace as well. If you work for a company and you are not a consumer of its goods and services, someone has to ask the hard questions around why.

The value proposition in this regard is not just how many of us are featured in advertising but what real impact do these companies have in our communities. The bottom line is that we should purchase products and goods from companies that have a presence in our communities and positively impacts the lives of people of color.

While I recognize that it is difficult to get insight into how companies embrace diversity in the workplace, as a prospective employee, you should perform some due diligence in terms of finding out how the company performs in this space. Going to a company's website, conducting research on the makeup of the Board; searching the web for any types of class action lawsuits; or just sitting outside the building when shop closes to observe the general makeup of those leaving for the day; can go a long way in determining where the company stands from a diversity perspective.

Chapter 7

Mentor Me

As I mentioned earlier, I benefited from some really good mentors early in my career who were mostly White. The advice was sound and got me off to a good start in pursuit of opportunities at work. The challenges that they could not relate to around race and cultural issues were addressed by family and friends who went through similar experiences climbing up the ladder.

While I appreciated the motivational input that I received from family, I often found it out of place with what I was dealing with at the time. Whenever I brought up some issue or challenge I faced at work there were a contingent of people who brought up the race card right away and suggested I sue or run to human resources versus those who sort of took the we shall overcome approach and urged me to suck it up and wait for a chance to escape.

Well meaning intentions aside, I tried to find other sources of guidance from more objective parties. I went to a major bookstore and looked in the management section for material on self development and career management. I counted over 125 titles that covered topics ranging from entry level dos and don'ts to step by step guidance on how to become a board member at a Fortune 500 company. Not one book spoke to career progression from the perspective of a person of color.

At around the same time I was seeking mentoring advice tailored to my background and experiences, my boss decided to call a meeting to acknowledge Black History and its importance to America.

While I sat in that meeting hoping that I would not be selected to be the spokesperson for Black America, it was only a matter of time before I was called out. She asked and then answered the question in one breath waiting for me to insert my opinion or position on the subject. The question went sort of something like this, "Why do we have all of these different magazines for men and women and people who are different, a magazine about health or beauty should just cover everyone instead of dividing people". "What does the group think, Gary?"

My response was fairly straight forward. I simply reminded her that many Black oriented periodicals and businesses for that matter were formed because of a lack of access to what was considered an exclusive club for the majority group. Her question was a brave one and I appreciated the fact that she posed it in front of all of us but I have encountered that scenario a few times too many in my career.

Blacks get a front row seat on race in this country and it is the one thing that we are experts on. Those who say we spend too much time focused on it are some of the same people who keep pushing it in our face. One day students at Rutgers University decided to play a joke on me by finding my home phone number in the directory and calling my mother at 1:00am on Martin Luther King Jr's birthday. They played a recording of his I have a dream speech and ad-libbed a few choice words and then hung up.

My mom called me, "are you ok" she asked. She spent the rest of the year worried about my safety at the school. More incidents followed, other students were harassed.

Managing your feelings about race and the impact that it has on opportunities will be more challenging than any work assignment that is thrown your way.

It is however, something that must be managed, conquered or stamped out of your psyche to avoid damaging your career aspirations. I have heard people say that we have a chip on our shoulder forever tied to what happened in the past bound by symbolic shackles that limit progress. Sure I agree some of us have a chip on our shoulder, but we didn't put it there. When every ethnic or immigrant group defines progress at the expense of your race, what the hell do you do about that?

The psychological impact of these issues takes its toll on progress in the corporate arena. Those of us who have managed to garner some slight degree of success in this space waste too much time fearful of the day the door will close or that open minded leader will move on to a new job and leave you hanging. After being frustrated for so many years overwhelmed with this idea that I was never good enough, I constantly worried that my work was wrong or would not be respected by others.

Moreover, I never had a true outlet or resource that I could sit down with and discuss what I was going through or what I was feeling. In some ways I was on my own. I had to mentor myself through many pitfalls relying mostly on instinct and advice from peers going through the same thing.

So many people that I knew had such a negative view of working in corporate America that they opted for government or nonprofit work. They gave up on the idea that they could be successful in this environment. While I managed to secure a few books written by Black CEOs that spoke to issues of race and work, I was unsuccessful in finding guidance that was aimed at advancement through the middle ranks of companies.

I decided to examine my strengths and weaknesses and decided to start with interviewing skills and job preparation as a point of focus. I decided that I would become the very best prospective employee that I could be. I wanted to knock their socks off during the interview process. Not an easy challenge since I was naturally shy and avoided social interaction at all costs.

Nevertheless I gave it a shot. I decided that I would interview at two companies a month even though I was happy in my current assignment. By honing my interviewing skills I hoped to get more comfortable discussing my qualifications and background while making contacts in the industry. That practiced worked. I was offered a number of jobs and eventually leveraged those contacts and secured better opportunities along the way. While money is a good thing it is not always a reason to make a move. I have also taken positions for less money with the intent of moving into a senior position in the long term.

In order to establish additional credibility during the interview process, you should bring a portfolio that highlights accomplishments and experiences that line up with what you say in your resume. For example, I had a recruiter who was so skeptical of my qualifications that he actually started writing equations on the board and testing me right in his office.

I am sure there were some issues of legality to that approach if he did not do that with other candidates. I always found myself on the receiving end of questions that sometimes would go on for hours; yes hours for an entry level managerial assignment.

In response to a few interviews gone wrong, if you will, I created a portfolio of work that lined up with my resume. For example, if I said that I led a project team of 20 people, my portfolio contained an organizational chart showing that I indeed had 20 directs reporting to me. If I referenced some toolkit or policy and procedure manual that I created, my portfolio had a sample of that information, as well. As I answered questions from interviewers, they were free to browse through the book as long as it stayed within my presence. The value proposition that I wanted to leave them with was "hire me and you can have the same thing", absent any proprietary information or trade secrets of course.

How many people simply walk into an interview hoping to win them over with a smile and a resume versus those who show pride in their accomplishments and work experience? The answer is that most people interviewing for jobs do the former.

You should look at your work experiences and output as portable and transferable even if you plan to work in a different industry. If you put together a slam dunk presentation and e-mailed it to your boss, you should add it to your portfolio stack for future reference. Start looking at the work you do as a bridge between your current and future assignments in the workplace.

Chapter 8

Crabs in a Barrel

Chances are if you are of working age and you happen to be Black you have heard the crabs in a barrel analogy a few million times. Pulling each other down just to get a leg up on everyone else is sort of what it means. I am sure that the analogy doesn't just ring true for people of color. Growing up in a rough and tough neighborhood in Paterson, New Jersey in the 70s and 80s I lived that analogy every day.

You see, I was the kid who took the back way home from school only to find out that the thugs were also waiting for me on the alternate path that became my personal underground railroad. My stops included the library, several alleys and quick exits out of the back of decoy buildings just to get home from school. Harriet Tubman would have been proud.

No matter how often I changed up the route, they always spotted me. Those crabs who just wanted me to be like them. Sometimes I had to literally fight my way home, I won some battles and I lost most but in the end I found something that helped me get through it all. I sort of invented a little motivational statement that helped me get through some of the nonsense and I said it every day I went to and from school. It went something like this, "they want you to be like them because they can't be like you, they want you to think like them because they can't think like you" and so on.

It did wonders for my psyche and unfortunately for many of those knuckleheads that chased me, they ended up in prison or 6 feet under. So what does this story have to do with moving you forward in your career? Trying to get to a better place can sometimes feel like you are abandoning your friends or peers who may look at work as just a job, not a career.

In some cases some people will accuse you of selling out or trying to be something other than Black. Since when has success and achievement been considered anti-Black? It's almost as if those concepts become kryptonite to Black folks because some of us believe that we shouldn't strive to be more main stream in our thinking regarding success and achievement.

In moving beyond such limited thinking we have to do so in a way that does not alienate the race or at least that's sort of what we have been indoctrinated into thinking. Frankly it's a tired old allegiance game that we have been placing on each other for a long time. It was tired in my college days and gets even more tiresome when I see it in the workplace. Imagine if we spent more time helping each other elevate ourselves to the next level as opposed to pursuing that virtual carrot that gets dangled out there for one or two of us to pursue.

Even the very concept of unity gets twisted by some who believe that it means that you have to follow the same belief pattern that they ascribe to or you risk vetoing your membership in the race. Succeeding in Corporate America does not require that you walk away from who and what you are. In fact, it is those very personal traits and characteristics that help to instill values and beliefs that can lead to a successful career.

Having a moral center, believing in the sanctity of family, working hard and demonstrating respect for yourself and others should be an intrinsic part of your belief system in all that you do. Any requirement that forces you to choose something else in exchange for some material gain probably isn't the right path to pursue. I find it much easier to stay true to your beliefs which will help you avoid some of the pitfalls and traps that await you in your assignments. Some people thrive on gossip and negativity in the workplace and all too often they expect you to do the same. We should not be prostituting our values for the sake of a raise or a promotion.

If you manage to stay centered you can deflect those vibes and stay focused on the work at hand. People will want you to choose sides and pledge your loyalty to them and not necessarily to what's in the best interest of the department or company. Unfortunately, there are those who will be afraid to stand up and express concern which is how companies get into trouble. They don't reinforce safe to say environments which caters to a culture of egocentricity and missed opportunities that interfere with strategic goals.

While I can't provide guidance on what to do when presented with ethical challenges or issues of conflict that challenge your sense of right and wrong, I can say that you must be grounded in all that you do. You didn't get this far by overcoming so many obstacles to now lose your sense of right and wrong. You can be morally centered and grounded and successful in a corporate climate but how you get there at times will be a struggle that you ultimately have to fight alone.

I can tell you that the less I focused on other people's issues, and the more I focused on ensuring that I performed my job responsibilities with the same sense of purpose that applied in my personal life, the happier I became. Don't worry about naysayers who say you can't do it, stay focused and in short order you will shake loose those crabs and make it out of the barrel.

At the end of the day you have to be able to envision where you want to be. You have to see it and feel it and know that it is possible to get there. You almost have to will it. If you can do that and stay the course, anything is possible. The world is changing and personal accountability will be the new mantra. Half hearted efforts and a preoccupation on what is wrong with someone else may have gotten folks an opportunity to advance in corporate America in the past but the tide is turning. The politics of deflection in the workplace must come to an end in order for Corporate America to remain a viable option for all.

While one might think that the crabs in a barrel analogy applies exclusively to one's racial group or makeup the reality is that the phenomenon is universal to all groups. If you can understand your environment you can anticipate some of the nonsense that others will throw your way. Unfortunately, it's the moments that we don't see coming that gets us into trouble. From the Manager who unintentionally insults you with compliments, to the latent racist who attempts to marginalize any and everything that you do.

While it is sometimes frustrating to deal with people who come off a certain way in the workplace, it can be beneficial to see those attitudes play out to their fullest. Being in the moment and learning adaptive ways to manage yourself through and out of those situations can strengthen your resolve.

Chapter 9

You Can Do This

One could rightfully argue that a lot of what we have discussed thus far applies to those who are already workforce eligible. People who have graduated from college and have some marketable skills to offer the workplace.

But what about those who didn't get an opportunity to even get that far? For example, people who have resolved themselves to a fate of accepting what life throws their way. I spoke about this earlier, the "we shall overcome" or day by day mentality that some of us ascribe to because we just can't see a way out.

The first step to getting on track towards getting to a better place is listing all the reasons why you think you can't on a sheet of paper. Double sided is ok but please limit it to one page. Write it all down. Bad father or mother, poor school district, no money just put it all on paper. Dropped out of high school, got pregnant or got someone else pregnant just make sure you get it all on paper. Review the list for 3 days and make sure you read each item out loud.

After 3 days take that list garble it up and throw it away. You just got rid of all the excuses on why you can't. Now let's focus on why you can. You can because you are here, you matter and the things that you want are within your reach. You have to see it and you have to believe it in order to make it a possibility.

Too many of us look to blame our misfortune on others. Maybe they deserve the blame but you should let them own that while you focus on owning the solutions that get you to where you want to be. If you are not willing to stand up for yourself and chart a different path, then why should anyone else be there to lend a helping hand? Sometimes we want someone else to own the solution, the plan and the outcome before we feel comfortable taking the first step. Step up and take charge of your life and own the outcomes.

I recall a bat wielding principal at my high school who was truly tough as nails when it came to disciplining students and teachers. I was familiar with Mr. Clark from my elementary schools years where he took names and kept prisoners. Students in detention looked like they were really being detained – in Russia.

I had unremarkable freshman and sophomore years at Eastside High School managing to maintain a B+ average and avoid getting attacked while I went from class to class. But I really came into my own my junior and senior year accomplishing a number of academic firsts for the school which got the eye of the principal.

I will never forget when the rankings came out and I ranked 47/450 graduating seniors that year. I thought that was a great accomplishment. That is, until I ran into Mr. Clark. "Garris" he said, "what happen with the rankings son?" he asked. "Why were you ranked so low?"

I looked him in the eye and I gave him the answer that he wanted to hear even though I didn't believe it at the time, "I didn't do my best sir" and he patted me on my back and told me to carry on in that drill like sergeant manner that he became known for at Eastside High.

Looking at that situation now, I realize that I could have done better. Sometimes we settle for less or sell ourselves short because we can't dare to dream beyond our reach. We are afraid to raise the bar for ourselves because we don't want to fail. Sometimes we go through life sort of seeking graded measures of success based on things that are attainable but don't really mean a whole lot. You know those superficial things that we can own, lease or rent that makes us feel like we are moving in the right direction when in all reality we keep taking steps backwards.

Some of us find our faith in God, an undeniable sense that our destiny is shaped by a divine power that has command over all things good and bad. So what will be will be, nothing less, nothing more, becomes the rationalize thought of eternal apathy and failure. But even God gave us independent thought and reasoning to seek a higher course which explains our continuous quest for a new and better existence. So make sure you apply the old adage that God helps those who help themselves as you plan for a better day.

While it's simple to say if you dream great things then great things will happen people have to extrapolate the thought into a customized roadmap that works for them. If you are a high school dropout and happen to be 40 years old, chances are you will never become a nuclear physicist. The odds are stacked against you. But if you apply some degree of realistic attainable goal setting that seeks improvement in your current circumstances then you are likely to succeed in overcoming the obstacles and excuses that have been in the way in the past.

So go into your HR department or speak to your boss about funding for community college or job training courses that map to your end goals. Employers will assist you in completing that GED or provide you with the opportunity to pursue an education that will lead to increased opportunity. Remember that the responsibility is yours to seek out a better destiny. You should not let anyone get in the way of those goals.

While success is a relative word, many of those who have "made it" often talk about pulling themselves up by their bootstraps which is analogous to not having a "thin dime" and the proverbial we were so poor that even the poor people looked down on us analogies of our parents. People recall those stories as examples of how anything is possible if you set your mind to it so use them for encouragement.

I tell those stories for a different reason. I tell them to remind myself to remember where I came from and to try and never ever end up there again. Make sure that in the course of inspiring others to do the right thing that you keep it real in terms of practical guidance and advice that is relevant to today. If we had it hard 2 or 3 decades ago, think how much crazier the world is for young people coming of age today. They really are dealing with what we dealt with compounded by a whole lot of other issues that can throw them off center much more quickly and harshly than what we encountered in our youth.

I guess that is the essence of what mentoring should really be about. Who wants a lecture about how great you are and how you made all the right choices when people are looking for answers that apply to their specific situation. Make sure that you provide your mentee with the stories of people who stuck their hands out to you to help you get there when your bootstrap was breaking.

Chances are the clergy, neighbors, friends in school, cousins etc. all helped you get to a better place unless you did it all by yourself. In fact, even the screw-ups helped by showing you the wrong things not to do so make sure you pay homage to all who helped along the way. After all, no one likes an arrogant mentor.

Chapter 10

Pretenders

Since I am attempting to coach you on some of the basics on moving up the proverbial career ladder I decided to remain as balanced as possible in my delivery. Now the gloves come off. Let's talk about the Pretenders. Not the singing group which was before your time and yes, before mine.

I am talking about leadership in a corporate setting. Pretenders are leaders who feign corporate affinity and responsibility to the detriment of the spirit of true corporate and personal accountability. Pretenders are good at dressing the part and looking the part but are usually poor at executing on delivery.

Now there are several types of pretenders all of whom usually bring some type of desirable skills to the table that usually get misapplied in some way or another. Here is a short list: <u>The Affinity Pretender</u>; <u>Pedigree Pretender</u>; and the <u>Bob and Weave Pretender</u>.

The Affinity Pretender is all about relationships. Every decision is made with the foresight of how to leverage the next opportunity for personal gain. While not necessarily a bad thing in and of itself, it sets the stage for wrong-headed business decisions that can have poor consequences if left unchecked.

When individuals make business decisions based on personality and relationships rather than on business objectives, the business loses. While the Pedigree Pretender may have lots of relationships, the one that counts is with the decision maker in the office, the "top dog", if you will.

This is the most dangerous pretender of all because he or she will exercise full discretion with the knowledge that the boss either does not care or will back them no matter the consequences.

Usually the Pedigree Pretender has an almost familial like relationship with the leader of the organization which can transcend into a literal one. I have seen the in-law come in and keep that connection quiet as they begin to usurp power quicker than a kid sucking up their favorite milk shake. Again, maybe the individual was qualified for the position and actually brings a great deal of value to the assignment but the direct line relationship to the leader presents challenges for all others down the line. Will you be brave enough to disagree? Will you revert to a yes man and equivocate at every step of the way? Probably, and that is why the Pedigree Pretender can get you and the company in a whole lot of trouble if you are not careful.

The Bob and Weave Pretender is the one that I have the most experience working with and what a challenge for those of you who have been fortunate enough to not encounter that type of leadership style. Suffice it to say the term leadership should be used loosely.

The Bob and Weave Pretender is all shine and gloss but is easily scratched and can be very high maintenance. They shun opportunities to step up and make a difference and opt for under the radar covert avoidance of all things of substance. They have a low tolerance for risks and usually do not have the cozy relationships of the pretenders I mentioned earlier.

Expect to be constantly deployed to help "sir or madam duck a lot" stay out of trouble. Don't expect to get any credit if you are successful because Bob and Weave will be right there standing on top of your work and claiming victory. Even Muhammad Ali in his prime would not be able to land a glove on good old Bob and Weave.

The real challenge in dealing with Pretenders and others with extreme leadership styles lies in how you choose to respond. Many of us give up out of frustration and try to find another job or allow our performance to suffer which results in termination.

Many of us get in trouble because we see the challenge in a negative context. Our defense mechanisms move us to react in a way that keeps us sort of in a zombie like work haze filled with tremendous amount of self doubt.

What if rather than defensively reacting to these situations you went on the offense. If the boss gave you a deadline of 2 weeks to get it done and you did it in 1 week. Imagine how great you'd feel about stepping up your game. If they yell at you for no justified reason, how about turning on the extra charm as an offensive response.

Instead of getting sidetracked and off course on achieving your objectives why not focus on staying the course. Also remember that there is a difference between Pretenders and tough challenging leaders who know their stuff. Don't run away from these leaders because they are the real deal, just like Evander Holyfield. Sorry, I happen to be a huge fight fan.

Take a look at various styles of leadership and attempt to emulate the good things that you see without adopting the bad. Sometimes I have to admit that I still get perplexed by some of the mean spiritedness I see in others at work. Someone once told me that I was not tough enough, that I had to yell more and carry on a bit to demonstrate that I was a good leader.

I guess that sort of explained why everyone on that team spent more time ripping others apart rather than focusing on the work at hand. I am confident that at some point in your career you will run into this old age smoke screen tactic that people use to divert attention away from what they are or are not doing in their shop.

Just remember, the best defense is truly a good offense and you will be fine. Don't get psyched out by barking dogs, just throw them a bone and get back on track with delivering the best work product possible.

There is absolutely nothing wrong with being collaborative in your approach to work assignments. Alienating others and being on the opposite side of partnering could lead to an early exodus from the company if you are not careful. While that hot headed ill tempered boss may be king for a day, adopting his or her style will leave you as a target when they move on and leave you to the peasants so be careful.

Chapter 11

Emotional Intelligence

In the previous chapter I touch on the challenge to keep your feelings in check and to not get drawn into a swarm of negative energy that may emanate from others. This is a very important skill-set to develop and based on my many discussions with women, it appears to be a big challenge for many of my colleagues who happen to be female.

That is not to say that men do not have the same challenges but many women that I have engaged in conversation with will openly talk about their inability to let the past stay in the past and that there is a tendency to never forget a transgression. As opposed to men who will deal with an issue and walk away and it's over.

I don't want to get into trouble by calling out what might be stereotypes so I will direct my comments to both genders. Try to avoid seeing a business challenge as a personal issue, yes it really is business and not personal. Individuals who are allowed to make it personal end up wasting time trying to draw blood as opposed to focusing on getting the work done.

Sometimes I have to remind coworkers that we work for shareholders and customers and the less time we spend thinking about how to provide excellent products and service, the more time our competitors have to fill that gap.

I often laugh at the silliness that I observe on a daily basis. People not speaking to each other or orchestrated attacks against associates who simply want to get the work done and go home.

Understand that not everyone wants a career. That does not mean that they are less vested in the success of completing work, it just means that their priorities are different.

You will certainly run into your control freaks, your "hey my title out ranks yours" and those nut jobs who will have a problem with you because well, It's you. I worked in a company that had a terrible reputation in the industry in terms of how they treated employees, especially new people coming into the organization. It was humorous to watch the old guard try and marginalize new people encouraging them to do less work so that they would not look bad. "There are no superstars", they would say, almost as if it was a threat.

Insecurity on full display these individuals went out of their way to prevent others from being successful. I love those kinds of environments because these folks help to validate just how good you are. After all if you are not getting reactions, then chances are you are not really adding value.

When people approach you with a high degree of skepticism or see you as a threat make sure that you stay above the fray. Sounds familiar? Emotional intelligence is about tempering your reactions in a measured and directed way to get to the desired business objectives at least in the short term. But what if you just come across that one person who seems intent in beating you up for the sport of it? Read on.

Chapter 12

Back Way Home Surviving Corporate Bullies

I grew up in a tough neighborhood in Paterson New Jersey where a high school principal had to carry a baseball bat to make a point. I have stared down the barrel of guns and survived a knife fight or two as I watched my childhood friends fall one by one to the hopelessness and misery that can so often be part of living in poverty.

While I've had my share of battles I also learned when it was time to take the back way home; that path around obstacles and challenges that may take a little longer, but can ultimately get you to your destination of choice. The same thing applies in the corporate arena. There is a time to fight and there is a time for avoidance and knowing the difference between the two can pave the way to success.

Corporate bullies dominate the landscape these days, embolden by pre-existing relationships and benefactors and filled with an overwhelming sense of entitlement and arrogance as they wreak havoc on your psyche and the environment around them.

I learned during my early years how to read and interpret behaviors very quickly. When your life is on the line and your next action can quickly become your last, you develop an innate ability to read and predict behavior in others.

Bullies also have that ability, they know who to pick on and they are aware of the scope and breadth of their reach into the organization. They succeed more times than not because you cannot fight back, the rules in the work place favor the bully, not you. Your recourse in those situations is to chart a path around the obstacle by taking the back way to your desired destination.

So here are some steps that you can take to ensure you have an alternate route:

1) Never become complacent in your current assignment. I cannot tell you how many times I have come across people who do not keep up to date resumes.

2) Use it. That resume is not just for self-affirmation. Interviewing internally and externally should be a part of your networking activities. Even if you have a cozy relationship with your boss it does not hurt to see what else is out there.

3) Don't get baited into the wrong reaction by someone else's insecurity. Take a step back refocus and engage individuals in a professional manner and do call them to the carpet when they cross the line

4) Contrary to some advice from an executive "taking it" is not a solution in the long run. I didn't survive all of those battles in the hood by not fighting back on occasion so don't just settle for silently walking away

Above all else, focus on doing an exemplary job in the face of the challenges thrown your way and be proactive in charting different paths around bullies. I promise you will get there if you avoid the dear in the headlights reaction to your current circumstances - so get moving.

Chapter 13

Toxic Individuals and Personality Disorders

There is a difference between bullies and toxic individuals and it's important to know the difference. Earlier we talked about ways to deal with bullies, or in some cases, when not to deal with them.

As pressure continues to increase in the job market with massive layoffs and a high unemployment rate, the impact on the American worker's psyche is taking a toll. Increasing incidences of workplace violence and higher incidences of mental and nervous disorders is partly attributed to these increasing pressures.

During my career I have had the unpleasant experience of working with people suffering from alcoholism, substance abuse and mental impairment. Challenges that I at least hope were not brought on by my work performance.

Kidding aside, it is difficult to work in high performance situations when you have an individual who is sort of adrift at sea without a sail or anchor.

Companies do not have good referral programs to help deal with these issues relying mostly on Employee Assistance Programs (EAPs) as opposed to self referral and reporting of individuals who may need to be approached for assistance.

I worked in an organization where a Senior Vice President had a history of poor relations with almost everyone in the organization except the President. This individual operated with reckless abandon and alienated everyone that crossed their path.

The difference between a bully and this type of individual is the way in which they choose to engage others. Each interaction is often personal as opposed to business focused. If there is a perception of a threat, then the impaired individual will often enter into extracurricular attempts to penalize individuals that do not agree with their position.

In many instances, the person does not have the ability to recall decisions that were previously made and will often draw the wrong conclusions about the work being done or assumptions about progress made to date.

This behavior will often result in you being thrown under the bus and will often keep you on the defensive. Many of us spend too much time in this space trying to make sense of the senseless. If you find yourself in a situation like this, you have to look at near term survival while developing a long term strategy to escape from the environment that you are in. In short order head for the hills. In the next chapter, I talk about steps that you can take to make that departure a little easier to pull off.

Chapter 14

How to Create a Golden Parachute

Face it. There will come a time when you will just have to walk away from the assignment end of story. The old days of 30 and 40 year careers are over.

If you have managed to do well, but have yet to reach that level in your career where you have a pre negotiated severance package. There are a couple of things that you can do to mimic the big boys and girls in building a safety net in case you need to exit stage left in your current assignment.

First, never ever stop updating the resume. Think of your resume as your passport, without it you will not be able to travel very far so keep it relevant and updated with the latest accomplishments and buzzwords.

Typical severance packages favor longevity which is quickly becoming a thing of the past so you will have to supplement that small severance package with 6 to 9 months of your net salary so start saving now. Do not rely on your 401k or retirement funds because you will end up paying a hefty toll to the IRS.

Sign on bonuses are not easy to negotiate however, companies are well aware that most senior managers are bonus eligible in the December to April range and the timing of payouts typically line up with recruiting and hiring spurts since budgets have been approved and departments start the recruiting process during the 1st quarter of the year. Try and time your pursuit to ensure that you can secure your bonus from your present employer which extends your savings and allows more time to pursue opportunities.

This may sound disingenuous but always keep your eye on the next job. Remember, that joining another company is like deciding to date someone new. It feels good at first because everyone is putting their best foot forward, but what if something goes wrong or you find out that you had too many blinders on in making the decision.

There is nothing wrong with having if then scenarios in case you find that the job you were promised, never existed. In short order, never take a job without having an idea of where the next one might come from.

Chapter 15

Attitude

At times throughout this book you will notice that I sort of walk a tightrope on some touchy issues around race and style in the workplace. One of the challenges that I am sure many of you deal with no matter what job or position you have, involves working for a boss who needs to constantly remind you that they are the boss. Of course this is a race neutral issue and probably impacts all of us at some point in our careers.

This is a tough one to get your arms around because there is not a whole lot you can do to change someone else's leadership style. We all want and need to feel like we are part of the solution and not the problem. But for leaders who talk at you and bark out orders while you take dictation, it can become a bit too much. Even when you try to provide input or contribute they cut you off and complete your idea or suggestion as if they want to prove that there is nothing that anyone else knows that they don't also have insight or perspective on.

How you deal with this depends on how thick your skin is and whether or not you can balance the work that needs to be done with the additional effort required to be submissive and subordinate yourself to your boss at all times. I remember the boss who once told me "I need you to participate in more meetings" only to give me the third degree at the next meeting when I suggested that we consider making a change in the existing workflow. This was one of those seen but not heard moments.

You should take stock of where you are and see if there really is a clear delineation of responsibility in your organization. Chances are if you and your peers are being micromanaged to death and second guessed at every step of the process then you probably have too many chiefs and not enough cooks. Waiting around for a change or trying to change the situation on your own might not be worthwhile.

Even if you advanced in this space and became part of the A team if you will, your new peers will expect you to adopt the same behavior, something that you probably would not be able to do, especially if you are reading this book.

Remember, getting there and staying there are two different animals that will require you to be adaptive and resourceful in ways that you probably have not prepared for.

People who have leadership roles in organizations make a lot of sacrifices which might account for some of the occasional attitude that you encounter. I have walked away from promotions or left jobs that required me to move to the next level where I thought I might have to make the wrong kinds of sacrifices. Figuratively, dogs bark when they hear other dogs bark and the rest of us react with fear and trepidation.

The key is to refocus on the short term objective of getting through the assignments and the longer term goal of getting to a better place. And remember attitude begets attitude so try and stay focused on meeting deliverables the best way you can and don't go home at the end of the day and bark at your family. Be in the moment.

Chapter 16

My History Does Not Have To Be Yours

Every mentor wants a different outcome for those that they guide, a better result than what they had. So we share our lessons learned as I have done in this book not because there is only a single path that can lead to the desired end goal. At least that is not why I decided to share my experiences with you.

I don't want you to be afraid to fail and I certainly don't want you to be afraid of success. Distracted by what you might think others are thinking about you. I also don't want you to question your capabilities or your intellect because of the perceptions or misguided notions of others.

I want you to be confident and comfortable in your skin. Approach your assignments with energy and confidence knowing that you will come out stronger in the end. Don't wait for a mentor to choose you, make the first move and try and build a focused relationship with someone who might have a vested interest in your success. Good people tend to want others to succeed. Some companies try and force those relationships with assigned mentors and while sometimes that can work, my experiences have resulted in a few lunch discussions and not a whole lot else. Forced interactions are hard to build relationships on so try to take the lead in making it happen.

Trying to get a seat at the table or be part of the club is not easy. Hard work alone does not get you there and I can tell you that I know what it's like to be part of the "A" team and I also know what it is like to be looking from the stands while the big hitters bat. It is always better to be swinging than sitting in the bleachers. There are usually no shortcuts to getting there for many of us and regimes in companies often change. Be patient and don't pursue disjointed and unconnected jobs that lead to nowhere.

The world is changing, becoming more and more multi-dimensional. What matters to us does not matter to our children. They are growing up together listening to the same music wearing the same clothes and being in the moment. Make sure that you are also in the moment in everything that you do.

Sure, we should never forget the past but not everyone is out to get you. The psychology of race can lead to isolation and a sort of self fulfilling prophecy that is difficult to escape from. If you are different, if you are looking through the window hoping that someone will open the door and let you in, go to the door and kick it in and let them know that you count, that you matter and that you will not go away. Stand up, be heard and be seen.

About the Author

A no nonsense discussion on the challenges of navigating through corporate challenges when you are on the outside looking in and wondering how you should deal with politics, toxic individuals and workplace challenges.

This is the mentor that you always wanted. Delivered with an entertaining and coach based style, this book will save you years of frustration by giving you the tools that you need to excel in the workplace. Written by Gary L. Garris, an Executive with over twenty years in the financial services industry working for major Fortune 500 companies and founder of Ventura Consulting, this book is the real deal.

Whether you are a seasoned veteran or new to the workplace there is something for everyone in this book. Gary addresses the taboo subject of race and challenges the reader to confront their own biases in dealing with issues and challenges of working together in a diverse environment.

His conversational delivery and tone comes at the right time as individuals are challenged to look at their work environment globally. This book takes those side conversations and water cooler talk about workplace difficulties and brings vital themes to the surface. Mentoring and guidance at its best, now all you have to do is be receptive to the guidance.

www.ingramcontent.com/pod-product-compliance
Lightning Source LLC
Chambersburg PA
CBHW050539280326
41933CB00011B/1652